# Race, Racism, and the Biblical Narratives

# Race, Racism, and the Biblical Narratives

On Use and Abuse of Sacred Scripture

## CAIN HOPE FELDER

FORTRESS PRESS
MINNEAPOLIS

Cover design: Marti Naughton

Cover image: https://commons.wikimedia.org/wiki/File:
Nubian_Tribute_Presented_to_the_King,_Tomb_of_Huy
_MET_DT221112.jpg Credit: Rogers Fund, 1930

Print ISBN: 978-1-5064-8852-3
eBook ISBN: 978-1-5064-8853-0

# Contents

# Contents

# Introduction

The aim of this essay is to discuss the questions of race and ethnic identity in the diverse biblical narratives. I hope to clarify, for modern readers, the profound differences in racial attitudes between those in the biblical world and in the subsequent history of Eurocentric interpretation. In antiquity, we do not have any elaborate definitions of or theories about race. This means that we must reckon with certain methodological problems in attempting to examine racial motifs as contained in the Bible. Ancient authors of biblical texts did have a color consciousness (awareness of certain physiological differences), but this consciousness of color/race, as we shall show, was by no means a political or ideological basis for enslaving, oppressing, or in any way demeaning other peoples.[1] In fact, the Bible contains no narratives in which the original intent was to negate the full humanity of black people or view blacks in an unfavorable way.[2] Such negative attitudes about black people are entirely postbiblical. In this regard, the following observation by Cornel West is most instructive:

> The very category of "race"—denoting primarily skin color—was first employed as a means of classifying human bodies by François Bernier, a French physician, in 1684. The first authoritative racial division of humankind is found in the influential *Natural System* (1735) of the preeminent naturalist Carolus Linnaeus.[3]

Indeed, theories that claim to provide a "scientific" basis for white racism are peculiar post-Enlightenment by-products of modern civilization.

The specific racial type of the biblical Hebrews is itself quite difficult to determine.[4] Scholars today generally recognize that the biblical Hebrews probably emerged as an amalgamation of races rather than from any pure racial stock. When they departed from Egypt, they may well have been Afro-Asiatics. To refer to the earliest Hebrews as "Semites" does not take us very far, inasmuch as the eighteenth-century term designates no race but a family of languages, embracing Hebrew, Akkadian, Arabic, as well as Ethiopic (*Ge'ez*).[5] The language of the ancient Ethiopians ("burnt-face" Africans), for example, is as Semitic as the language of early Hebrews (Jahwists), or of the Arabs.[6] This reaffirms the contention that sophisticated theories about race and the phenomenon of racism are cultural trappings that appear well after the biblical period. Consequently, the task at hand is to construct an interpretative framework for a range of biblical attitudes about race and to determine implications for the postbiblical problems of racism and ethnocentrism that continue to bedevil both church and society in many nations today, including those of the Third World. There is still too much sad evidence of the dominant classes within Third World nations imitating oppressive racial/ethnic patterns of their former European colonizers.

Although the Bible primarily presents sociopolitical entities that are differentiated as empires, nations, and tribes, there are important ways in which the subject of race acquires particular significance. This essay will examine the thesis that in the biblical corpus, two broad processes related to racism may be operating. First, there is the phenomenon of *sacralization*. By this I mean the transposing of an ideological concept into a tenet of religious faith (or a theological justification) in order to serve the vested interest of a particular ethnic/racial group. Second, there is the process of *secularization*: the weakening of a powerful religious concept under the weighty influence of what today we call "secular" (i.e., sociopolitical and ideological) pressures.[7] In this second process, ideas are wrenched from their original religious moorings due to the weighty influence of nationalistic ideologies and cultural understandings. This is not to say that the process of sacralization or secularization was a conscious design on the part of ancient biblical writers. On the contrary, I only suggest that the process was circumstantial and subtle. It becomes problematic when the meaning of ancient texts assumes a normative character centuries later. The phenomena of sacralization and secularization often cultivate patterns of ethnocentrism and even racism that in turn can have harmful effects on certain racial and ethnic groups who are inevitably scorned and marginalized.

# Race and Sacralization in the Old Testament

Several Old Testament passages are quite suitable as illustrations of sacralization and as such require a new kind of critical engagement. First, I shall consider the so-called curse of Ham (Gen. 9:18–27), which rabbis of the early Talmudic periods and the church fathers, at times, used to demean black people. Later Europeans adopted the so-called curse of Ham as a justification for slavery and stereotypical aspersions about blacks. Second, I will focus on the Old Testament genealogies that contributed to the Israelites' and ancient Jews' perception that they implicitly constituted a most divinely favored people ("race"). Third, I shall discuss the fascinating narrative about Miriam and Aaron, who objected to Moses's Ethiopian wife (Num. 12:1–16). Fourth, I shall take up the explicit biblical doctrine of election (i.e., of a chosen people) as it developed as a theme in the Old Testament; my discussion of that theme will conclude with a brief comparison of the Old Testament's and New Testament's handling of the doctrine.

# The Curse of Ham

My first example of sacralization occurs in some of the earliest Jahwist (J) traditions of the Old Testament. Genesis 9:18–27 has achieved notoriety in many quarters because it contains the so-called curse of Ham. The passage technically should follow directly upon the J passage that concludes the flood narrative (Gen. 8:20–22), since critical investigations have shown that Genesis 9:1–17 and verses 28–29 represent the much later Priestly (P) exilic tradition.[1] The great significance of Genesis 9:18–27 is not that it contains the so-called curse of Ham (which technically does not take place at all); rather, it is that these verses make it clear that to the mind of the ancient Israelite author, "the whole post-diluvial humanity stems from Noah's three sons."[2] On Genesis 9:19, Claus Westermann remarks as follows:

The whole of humankind takes its origin from them [Shem, Ham, Japheth]. . . . Humanity is conceived here as a unity, in a way different from the creation; humanity in all its variety across the earth, takes its origin from these three who survived the flood. The purpose of the contrast is to underscore the amazing fact that humanity scattered in all its variety throughout the world comes from the one family.[3]

Once the passage establishes the perception about this essential and fundamental aspect of human origin (vv. 18–19), it continues by providing what appears to be a primeval rationale for differences in the destinies or fortunes of certain groups of persons. Certainly, as one scholar notes, "from a form critical viewpoint Genesis 9:20–27 is an ethnological etiology concerned with the theology of culture and history."[4] This observation alerts us to the theological motives in verses 20–27 that have implications for definite construals of both culture and history. In my view, it is this development that most clearly attests to the process of sacralization, wherein cultural and historical phenomena are recast as theological truths with vested interest for particular groups.

Prior to delineating some of the internal difficulties and other features of Genesis 9:18–27, a word may be said about the literary form of this narrative. The narrative passages of Genesis 1–11 generally concern the matter of "crime and punishment: this is particularly evident in the ('J') narratives."[5] Westermann informs us that these narratives have antecedents and parallels in ancient African myths: "It is beyond dispute that African myths about the primeval state and biblical stories of crime and punishment in J correspond both in their leading motifs and in their structure."[6] African and African American scholars have reached similar conclusions.[7] With respect to Genesis 9:18–27, the crime is Ham's allowing himself to see the nakedness of his drunken father, Noah, without immediately covering him. In error, Ham leaves his father uncovered (according to Hebrew tradition, an act of great shamelessness and parental disrespect) while he goes to report on Noah's condition to Shem and Japheth, his brothers (v. 22). For their part, Ham's two brothers display proper respect in meticulous ways as they cover their father (v. 23). When Noah awakens (v. 24), the problems begin. Noah pronounces a curse not upon Ham, but upon Canaan, who has not been mentioned previously. Noah also blesses Shem and Japheth, presumably as a reward for their sense of paternal reverence as demanded in ancient Hebrew tradition.

If one attempts to argue for the unity of the passage, inconsistencies and other difficulties abound. To illustrate, Ham commits the shameless act in verse 22, but Canaan is cursed in verse 25. In Genesis 9:18, the list of Noah's sons refers to Ham as being second, but in verse 24, the text, presumably referring to Ham, uses the phrase Noah's "youngest son." Also, the mention of Canaan as cursed in verse 25 raises the possibility, albeit slightly untenable, that Noah had a fourth son so named. Then too, uncertainties about the precise nature of Ham's error have resulted in a fantastic variety of suggestions about the incident: it has been suggested that Ham possibly castrated his father, that he sexually assaulted his father, that he committed incest with his father's wife, and that he had sexual relations with his own wife while aboard the Ark.[8] As I have suggested, the matter was far less complicated, for Ham violated the sacred rule of respect for his father. Many of the difficulties within this passage find a solution once we allow the possibility that the original version of Genesis 9:18–27 referred only to Ham and his error and that a later version of the story, motivated by political developments in ancient Palestine, attempted to justify the subjugation of Canaanites by Shem's descendants (Israel) and those of Japheth (Philistines).[9]

While admitting the passage's contradiction that it is Ham who shows disrespect to Noah but Canaan, Ham's son, who is cursed, Westermann asserts,

The same person who committed the outrage in verse 22 falls under the curse in verse 25. The Yahwist has preserved, together with the story of Ham's outrage, a curse over Canaan which could be resumed because of the genealogical proximity of Canaan to Ham. Those who heard the story knew the descendants of Ham as identical with those of Canaan.[10]

Thus, in Westermann's view, Ham, in effect, *was* cursed and presumably with him not just Canaan but all of the other descendants of Ham—that is, Cush, Egypt, and Put (Phut), as cited in Genesis 10:6. Although I disagree with Westermann's contention that Ham was, *in effect*, cursed in Genesis 9:18–27, Westermann does help us see that the ambiguity of the text can lead Bible interpreters to justify their particular history, culture, and race by developing self-serving theological constructs. In one instance, the Canaanites "deserve" subjugation; in another instance, the Hamites "deserve" to be hewers of wood and drawers of water.

Whether or not sacralization was ever part of the original narrative of the error of Ham, we have much evidence of such sacralization in the Midrashim—for example, in the fifth-century (CE) Midrash, in which Noah says to Ham, "You have prevented me from doing something in the dark [cohabitation], therefore your seed will be ugly and dark-skinned."[11] Similarly, the Babylonian Talmud (sixth century CE) states that "the descendants of Ham are cursed by being Black and are sinful with a degenerate progeny."[12] Into the seventeenth century, the idea persisted that the blackness of Africans was due to a curse, and that idea reinforced and sanctioned the enslavement of blacks.[13] Indeed, even today, in such versions of Holy Scripture as *Dake's Annotated Reference Bible*, one finds at Genesis 9:18–27 a so-called great racial prophecy with the following racist hermeneutic:

> All colors and types of men came into existence after the flood. All men were white up to this point, for there was only one family line—that of Noah who was white and in the line of Christ, being mentioned in Luke 3:36 with his son Shem. . . . [There is a] prophecy that Shem would be a chosen race and have a peculiar relationship with God [v. 26]. All divine revelation since Shem has come through his line. . . . [There is a] prophecy that Japheth would be the father of the great and enlarged races [v. 27]. Government, Science and Art are mainly Japhethic. . . . His descendants constitute the leading nations of civilization.[14]

# Old Testament Genealogies

Another instance of sacralization confronts us quite early in the Old Testament within the genealogies of the descendants of Noah. It is especially useful to consider the so-called Table of Nations (Gen. 10) in conjunction with the much later genealogical listing of 1 Chronicles 1:1–2:55. On the one hand, these listings purport to be comprehensive catalogs. All too often the general reader erroneously has taken these catalogs to be reliable sources of ancient ethnography. Critical study of these genealogies illuminates theological motives that inevitably yield an increasing tendency to arrange different groups in priority, thereby attaching the greatest significance to the Israelites as an ethnic and national entity, greater than all other peoples of the earth. I shall first examine the deceptive quality of these Old Testament genealogies and then—after discussing the narrative regarding Miriam and Aaron—will show how their evident sacralization parallels yet another instance of this phenomenon: namely, the whole notion of election (of a chosen people).

While at first glance Genesis 10 has the appearance of being a single listing of ancient nations, biblical criticism has for some time demonstrated that Genesis 10 represents a conflation of at least two different lists—that is, the Jahwist (J) and the Priestly (P)—separated by centuries.[1] In fact, the conflation of different traditions in Genesis 10 doubtlessly accounts for matters such as the discrepancies in identifying the land of Cush, discrepancies in determining the relationship between Cush and Sheba, and the differences between Seba and Sheba. For example, Genesis 10:7 mentions Seba (*sĕbʾā*) as a son of Cush, whereas Sheba (*šĕbʾā*) is a grandson of Cush according to Genesis 10:8. Here the text clearly is identifying the descendants of Ham (*ḥām*). Then in Genesis 10:28, the text introduces an anomaly, since, at this point, Sheba is mentioned as a direct descendant not of Ham but of Shem. Furthermore, since the initial Samech (*s*) of *sĕbʾā* is the equivalent of and interchangeable with the Hebrew Shin (*š*) in Old South Arabic,[2] one could argue that Genesis 10 offers us two persons named Sheba as descendants of Cush, but only one person by that name as a descendant of Shem. In any case, the Table of Nations as it stands does not delineate sharp racial differences between the ancient peoples of Africa, South Arabia, and Mesopotamia. The true motive lies elsewhere.

Rather than any objective historical account of genealogies, the Table of Nations in Genesis 10 presents us with a theologically motivated catalog of people. The table not only ends with the descendants of Shem but does so in a way consciously stylized to accentuate the importance of the descendants of Shem among the peoples of the earth.[3] About this, the author of the genealogy in 1 Chronicles 1:17–34 is most explicit, inasmuch as of all the descendants of the sons of Noah, those descended from Shem receive the most elaborate attention. Thus, the Jahwist listing of the nations is the most primitive; the list in Genesis 10 was composed centuries later and was edited theologically according to a postexilic Priestly tradition in order to establish the priority of the descendants of Shem; that list was followed by a further elaboration, centuries later, found in the genealogies of 1 Chronicles. In this long progression, the theological presuppositions of a particular ethnic group displace any concern for objective historiography and ethnography. The descendants of Noah apart from those of Shem are increasingly insignificant and gain access to the text only as they serve as foils to demonstrate the priority of Israelites.

The subtle process being described may consequently be called "sacralization" because it represents an attempt on the part of succeeding generations of one ethnic group to construe salvation history in terms distinctly favorable to it as opposed to others. Here, ethnic particularity evolves with a certain divine vindication, and inevitably the dangers of rank racism lie just beneath the surface. Gene Rice has noted rightly that the genealogies do not express negative attitudes about persons of African descent, but it is important to clarify an aspect of Rice's judgment in light of the way in which sacralization nevertheless expresses itself in these genealogies. Consider Rice's remarks:

> Genesis 10 has to do with all the peoples of the world known to ancient Israel and since this chapter immediately follows the episode of Noah's cursing and blessing, it would have been most appropriate to express here any prejudicial feelings toward African peoples. Not only are such feelings absent, but all peoples are consciously and deliberately related to each other as brothers. *No one, not even Israel, is elevated above anyone else and no disparaging remark is made about any people, not even the enemies of Israel.*[4]

It is necessary to qualify Rice's contention that the genealogies do not elevate even Israel above any other people. After all, Genesis 10:21–31 becomes the basis for amplifying in great detail the descendants of Shem and Judah (1 Chron. 2:1–55) as the distinctive *laos tou Theou* ("people of God," LXX). Thus these genealogies are construed theologically to enhance the status of a particular people ("race"), and this is precisely the process that I am describing as sacralization.

# The Narrative about
# Miriam and Aaron

Numbers 12:1–16 may also attest to a process of moving from ethnic particularity to a kind of sacralized ethnocentrism with certain class implications. In Numbers 12:1, Moses's brother (Aaron) and sister (Miriam) castigate him for having married a Cushite (i.e., "Ethiopian") woman (*hā'iŝā hacūŝiṯ*). Several factors point to the probability that the offensive aspect of the marriage was the woman's black identity. In the first place, this is clearly the view expressed in the wording of the Septuagint: *heneken tēs gunaikos tēs Aithopisses* (on account of the Ethiopian woman).[1] Second, God visits leprosy upon Miriam as a punishment (v. 9), and it can hardly be accidental that Miriam is described as "leprous, as white as snow." Quite an intentional contrast is dramatized here: that is, Moses's black wife, accursed by Miriam and Aaron, is now contrasted with Miriam, who suddenly becomes "as white as snow" in her punishment. The contrast is sharpened all the more since only Miriam is punished for an offense in which Aaron is equally guilty. The testimony of the Septuagint together with these exegetical considerations points strongly to the probability that more than arrogance is at issue in this text. Also involved is a rebuke to the prejudice characterized by the attitudes of Miriam and Aaron.

In the Numbers 12 narrative, God sternly rebukes Miriam and Aaron, but the central question is, Why? The ambiguities of this narrative abound. Is God's rebuke the result of the presumptions of Miriam and Aaron to question Moses's decision no matter whom he married? Is God's censure caused by the fact that the black wife of Moses is a foreigner (from Ethiopia/Nubia = present-day Sudan)? Or may it be the case, as Randall Bailey suggested in a recent conversation with me, that the black identity of Zipporah indeed may be pertinent, but not for the reasons that I offered in chapter 3 of *Troubling Biblical Waters*?[2] As a rejoinder to my published argument, Bailey surmised that not only did those in the ancient world regard black Africans favorably, but at times, they became the standard by which others judged themselves. In chapter 8 of *Stony the Road We Trod: African American Biblical Interpretation*, Bailey develops this idea of "valorization" in relation to ancient Israel's self-esteem and black Africans. In Bailey's line of reasoning, God's rebuke had more to do with attitudes of class in relation to race than with matters of religion. The jealousy of Moses's relatives stemmed from his marriage to a woman of *higher* social standing than the Hebrews themselves, who were of mixed Afro-Asiatic stock.[3] If Bailey is correct, his idea of class bias would thereby account for the anomaly of having only this text in the Bible exhibiting some bias *against* a black, as I had earlier intimated. This is a perennial reminder that the racial values of the Bible are progressive in comparison to later hostile racial attitudes in the medieval and modern periods.[4] The Numbers 12 narrative exposes the contrast between the biblical world before color prejudice and our postbiblical Western history of translation and interpretation that have marginalized blacks in antiquity while sacralizing other groups.

The process of sacralization in the Old Testament inescapably involves certain racial ambiguities. For example, Eurocentric Bible translators and interpreters over the years routinely have considered the mixed stock of ancient Afro-Asiatics as somehow "nonblack." This academic "sleight of hand" becomes most apparent when one then finds that in places such as the United States of America, the racial classification of a person as black is made on the basis of the most minuscule amount of traceable African descent. Thus, we arrive at the utter absurdity where in the United States, mulattos/coloreds are considered Negro/black; whereas in South Africa or Brazil, the same racially mixed peoples attain, as nonblacks, higher social standing than those who have more pronounced traditionally black African features. By contrast, when we turn to the Hebrew Scriptures, the ancient authors there tend to distinguish ethnic identity solely on the basis of tribes or nationality. The distinction that the Old Testament makes is not racial. Through the process of sacralization, a principle of exclusion or prioritization is indeed present—all who do not meet the criteria for salvation as defined in the Old Testament are relegated to an inferior status. However, that exclusion is not based upon race but rather upon not being a part of the ethnic or national "in-group." This is the reason that black people are not only frequently mentioned in numerous Old Testament texts but are also mentioned in ways that are most favorable in terms of acknowledging their actual and potential role in the salvation history of Israel. By no means are black people excluded from the particularity of Israel's story as long as they claim it, however secondarily, and do not proclaim their own story apart from the activity of Israel's God.

Extensive lists of Old Testament passages that make favorable reference to black people are readily accessible.[5] There are many illustrations of such provocative texts. Isaiah 37:9 and 2 Kings 19:9 refer to Tirhakah, king of the Ethiopians. This ancient black Pharaoh was actually the third member of the twenty-fifth Egyptian dynasty, which ruled all of Egypt (689–664 BCE).[6] According to the biblical texts, Tirhakah was the object of the desperate hopes of Israel; in the days of Hezekiah, Israel hoped desperately that Tirhakah's armies would intervene and thus stave off an impending Assyrian assault by Sennacherib. More than a half-century later, another text could refer to "the mighty men of Ethiopia and Put who handle the shield" (Jer. 46:9). Indeed, the Old Testament indicates that black people were part of the Hebrew army (2 Sam. 18:21–32) and even part of the royal court. The *'Ebed-melek* takes action to save Jeremiah's life (Jer. 38:7–13) and thereby becomes the beneficiary of a singular divine blessing (Jer. 39:15–18). The dominant portrait of the Ethiopians in the Old Testament is that of wealthy people (Job 28:19; Isa. 45:14) who would soon experience conversion (Ps. 68:31; Isa. 11:11; 18:7; Zeph. 3:10). The reference to "Zephaniah, son of Cush" (Zeph. 1) may indicate that one of the books of the Old Testament was authored by a black African.[7]

# The Doctrine of Election

Israel's particularity, as considered in the foregoing discussions of race and sacralization, loses much of its subtlety as the dubious concept of its election (*bāḥar*) begins to gain a firm footing in the Old Testament. Certainly, traces of the idea of Israel's chosenness and special relationship with its deity were present in "the pre-Jahwistic cult of the ancestors," but the explicit concept of Jahweh's loving preference for the people of Israel develops relatively late.[1] The theologically elaborate belief that Jahweh specifically chose Israel above all other nations does not become a matter of religious ideology and hence an instance of sacralization until the period of Deuteronomistic history toward the end of the seventh century BCE (Deut. 7:6–8; 10:15; Jer. 2:3; cf. Isa. 43:20; 65:9).[2]

Regardless of the theological structure that attempts to support the Deuteronomistic concept of Israel's election, ambiguities almost immediately engulf the concept. Horst Seebass, for example, insists that even among the Deuteronomistic writers, Israel's election "only rarely stands at the center of what is meant by election."[3] According to him, *bāḥar*, as a technical term for Israel's election, always functions as a symbol of universalism; that is, it represents Israel in the role of "service to the whole."[4] Seebass is representative of those who want to de-emphasize the distinctive ethnic or racial significance of the concept in Israel's self-understanding in the Deuteronomistic period.[5]

The ethnic and racial ambiguities involved in the concept of Israel's election seem to persist, albeit with many rationales to the contrary. The ambiguity does not so much result from the fact that a universalistic history is presupposed by the biblical writers who advance the Old Testament concept of Israel's election; rather, the ambiguities stem from the nature of the so-called universalism that is presupposed. Gerhard von Rad points out that in the Deuteronomistic circles, the chosenness of Israel attains a radical form and its universal aspect is at best paradoxical.[6] I would further suggest that perhaps the real paradox resides in the notion that Israel's election in a universal divine scheme seems to lead inevitably to sacralization, with the people of Israel as an ethnic group at the center. Certainly, the Deuteronomistic authors struggled to demonstrate Jahweh's singular affirmation of the Davidic monarchy and, more importantly, Jahweh's selection of Jerusalem as the center of any continuing redemptive activity.[7] Again, it seems quite paradoxical that, although the people of Israel exhibit few extraordinary attributes or values by which they objectively merit Jahweh's election, there develops, particularly in postexilic Judaism, an elaborate doctrine of merit by which those who know and follow the Torah within Israel as an ethnic group attempt to prove their worthiness as the chosen people.

Despite the absence of any inherent superiority of the people of Israel in their lengthy biblical documentary of their own sin and instances of faithlessness, the concept of election becomes inextricably bound up with ethnic particularity. Accordingly, the people of Israel arrogate to themselves the status of being preeminently chosen and thereby claim to possess the Law and the covenant and a continuing promise of the land and the city. At the same time, all who stand outside the community or apart from the supporting religious ideology of election are relegated to the margins of Israel's "universal" saving history. In this progression, as we have seen, other races and ethnic groups may, of course, subscribe to Israel's religious ideology and derive the commensurate benefits, but always the criteria for such subscription seem to be mediated through the predilections of an ethnic group reinforced by elaborate genealogies and the transmission of particular legal religious traditions.

This development typifies what I have called the process of sacralization, and it is striking to see the different way that New Testament authors treat the doctrine of election. The Old Testament scholar George Foot Moore provides us with a glimpse of the different conception that one encounters in the New Testament; he asserts that, for the Old Testament idea of national election, "Paul and the church substituted an individual election to eternal life, without regard to race or station."[8] Rudolf Bultmann provides us with a more helpful understanding of the New Testament in this regard. He argues that, in the New Testament, the Christian church becomes "the true people of God"; in Bultmann's view, the New Testament no longer concerns itself with a preeminent ethnic group—that is, *Israēl kata sarka* (1 Cor. 10:18), but with the Israel of God (Gal. 6:16) without any exclusive ethnic or racial coordinates.[9]

In contrast to the Deuteronomistic usage of *bāḥar*, the New Testament never presents the term *eklegomai* or its nominal derivatives *eklektos* (chosen) and

*eklogē* (election) in an ethnically or racially restric-
tive or exclusive sense. Paul wants to maintain a certain continuity with aspects of Israel's election in the
Old Testament, but that continuity is neither ethnic
nor cultic (Rom. 9:11; 11:2, 11, 28–29). For Paul, corporate election can include some Jews, but it must
also embrace Gentiles (Rom. 11:25; Gal. 3:28; 1 Cor.
12:13); being "in" and "with" Christ becomes the new
*crux interpretum*. In Paul's view, God chose (*exelexato*) the foolish, weak, and low (1 Cor. 1:27–28). For
James, God chose (*exelexato*) the poor who are rich
in faith (James 2:5); for Matthew, God calls many but
chooses only the few (Matt. 22:14). The new universalism and unity to be found in the Christian church
express themselves further in the new sequence of
thoughts found in Galatians 3:28 ("There is neither
Jew nor Greek, there is neither slave nor free, there is
neither male nor female; for you are all one in Christ
Jesus"); 1 Corinthians 12:13 ("For by one Spirit we
were all baptized into one body—Jews or Greeks,
slaves or free—and all were made to drink of one
Spirit"); and Colossians 3:11–12 ("Here there cannot
be Greek and Jew, circumcised and uncircumcised,
barbarian, Scythian, slave, free man, but Christ is
all, and in all").

The only New Testament text that refers to Chris-
tians as a chosen race (*genos eklekton*) is 1 Peter 2:9.

Yet in the text of 1 Peter, the phrase is manifestly metaphorical. The text depends very heavily on the wording found in Isaiah 43:20–21 (LXX), but the ethnic particularity implied in the Old Testament text has fallen away entirely in 1 Peter.[10] Thus, in Christian literature throughout the New Testament period (which extends well into the second century), the elect become the church, which is the new Israel. Matthew is even more specific because for him the elect represent the faithful few in the church who accept the call to the higher righteousness and the doing of the will of God. In either case, these New Testament perspectives eliminate all ethnic or racial criteria for determining the elect.[11]

# Secularization in the New Testament

Ambiguities with regard to race in the New Testament do not appear within the context of what I have defined as sacralization. Accordingly, I have tried to show that the New Testament disapproves of an ethnically focused idea of corporate election (or "Israel according to the flesh"). In fact, the New Testament offers no grand genealogies designed to sacralize the myth of any inherent and divinely sanctioned superiority of Greeks and Romans in any manner comparable to the Table of Nations found in Genesis 10. Further, many Palestinian Jews of Jesus's time could be easily classified as Afro-Asiatics, despite the fact that European artists and American mass media have routinely depicted such persons as Anglo-Saxons. Indeed, Matthew, Mark, and Luke report that an African helped Jesus carry his cross (Matt. 27:32; Mark 15:21; Luke 23:26; contra John 19:17).

Consequently, if one is to explore the subject of racialist tendencies in the New Testament narratives, one must turn to a different phenomenon—namely, the process of secularization. The question now becomes, How did the expanding church, in its attempt to survive without the temporary protection it derived by being confused with Judaism, begin to succumb to the dominant symbols and ideologies of the Greco-Roman world? We will want to see how, in this development, the universalism of the New Testament circumstantially diminishes as Athens and Rome become substituted for Jerusalem of the Old Testament, as, in effect, the new centers for God's redemptive activity.

The conceptualization of the world by early Christian authors of New Testament times scarcely included Sub-Saharan Africa and did not at all include the Americas or the Far East. These early Christian writers referred to Spain as "the limits of the West" (1 Clem. 5:7; Rom. 15:28); they envisioned the perimeters of the world as the outer reaches of the Roman Empire.[1] For New Testament authors, Roman sociopolitical realities as well as the language and culture of Hellenism often arbitrated the ways in which God was seen as acting in

Jesus Christ. Just as Jerusalem in the Old Testament had come to represent the preeminent holy city of the God of Israel (Zion), New Testament authors attached a preeminent status to Rome, the capital city of the world in which an increasingly Gentile church was emerging.[2]

It is no coincidence that Mark, probably the earliest composer of the extant passion narratives, goes to such great lengths to show that the confession of the Roman centurion (only here the Latinism *kentyrion* [*centurio*] in the Synoptic passages) brings his whole gospel narrative to its climax.[3] For his part, Luke expends considerable effort to specify the positive qualities of his various centurions (*hekatont-arches*).[4] There is even a sense in which their official titles symbolize Rome as the capital of the Gentile world, for their incipient acts of faith or confessions, according to Luke, find their dénouement in the Acts 28 portrait of Paul, who proclaims relentlessly the kerygma in Rome. The immediate significance of this New Testament tendency to focus upon Rome instead of Jerusalem is that the darker races outside the Roman orbit are circumstantially marginalized by New Testament authors.

For lack of more descriptive terminology, this process by which the darker races are marginalized in the New Testament may be called secularization.

Here, sociopolitical realities of the secular framework tend to dilute the New Testament vision of racial inclusiveness and universalism. In order to expose this process, one must examine early traditions and show how they were adapted at later stages in such a way as to be slanted to the detriment of the darker races. Perhaps one of the most cogent illustrations of this process of secularization is Luke's narrative about the baptism and conversion of the Ethiopian official in Acts 8:26–40.

On the surface, Acts 8:26–40 is a highly problematic text. One wonders immediately if the Ethiopian finance minister of the *kandakē* (the Queen of Nubia/biblical Ethiopia with her capital at Meroë) is a Jew or Gentile. One also wonders about the efficacy of the finance minister's baptism and whether it constituted or led to a full conversion to Christianity. Probably the best survey of the several problems posed by this pericope is that by Ernst Haenchen, who entitles the pericope "Philip Converts a Chamberlain."[5] According to Haenchen, Luke is intentionally ambiguous about the Ethiopian's identity as a Gentile or Jew—Luke merely appeals to this conversion story in order to suggest "that with this new convert the mission has taken a step beyond the conversion of Jews and Samaritans."[6] The story itself derives from Hellenistic circles and represents for Luke, in Haenchen's view, a parallel and rival to Luke's own account of Cornelius as the first Gentile convert under the auspices of Peter.[7] Haenchen detects no particularly significant racial difficulties posed by Acts 8:26–40. For him, Luke merely edits this Hellenistic tradition to conform to his own theological design.

Today there are those who tend to exclude black people from any role in the Christian origins, and they need to be reminded that quite possibly a Nubian was the first Gentile convert.[8] Nonetheless, Luke's awkward use of this story seems to have certain racial implications. Notice that in Acts 8:37, the Ethiopian says, "See, here is some water! What is to prevent me from being baptized?" A variant reading immediately follows in some ancient manuscripts of the text (i.e., "And Philip said, 'If you believe with all your heart, you may [be baptized].' And he [the Ethiopian] replied, 'I believe that Jesus Christ is the Son of God'").[9] Whether or not one accepts this variant reading as an authentic part of the text, it is clear that the Ethiopian's baptism takes place in the water without reference to a prior or simultaneous descent of the Holy Spirit (cf. John 3:5; 1 John 5:6–8). By contrast, Luke provides an elaborate narrative about Cornelius's conversion and baptism (Acts 10:1–48), at the end of which the Holy Spirit descends and the baptism by water follows. Furthermore, Peter's speech (Acts 10:34–43) indicates a new development in which Gentiles are unambiguously eligible for conversion and baptism. Given the importance of the Holy Spirit's role throughout Luke–Acts as a theological motif, Luke's narrative about Cornelius's baptism unwittingly gives the distinct impression that Cornelius's baptism is more legitimate than that of the Ethiopian.

I, by no means, want to suggest that Luke had a negative attitude toward black people. On the contrary, one need only consider the list of the Antiochene church leadership that Luke presents in Acts 13:1 to dispel such notions. There Luke mentions one "Simeon who is called the black man" (*Symeon ho kaloumenos Niger*). The Latinism here (i.e., *Niger*) probably reinforces the idea that Simeon was a dark-skinned person, probably an African.[10] Luke's vision was one of racial pluralism in the leadership of the nascent Christian church at Antioch (Acts 11:26). Furthermore, I hasten to add that in no way do I think it important or useful to dwell on the point that the first Gentile convert was quite possibly a Nubian as opposed to an Italian. This would be absurd, of course, given the confessional nature of the entire Luke–Acts corpus, which does not come to us as objective history. The racial implication that I do wish to highlight is that Luke's editorializing results in a circumstantial de-emphasis of a Nubian (African) in favor of an Italian (European) and enables Europeans thereby to claim that the text of Acts demonstrates some divine preference for Europeans.

Beyond this merely circumstantial de-emphasis of that which is African, it seems that Luke's literary scheme in the Acts of the Apostles falls prey to secular ideologies. His possible apologetics for a Roman provincial official (Theophilus) as well as the great significance that he attaches to Rome as the center of the world contribute to this (see Luke 1:3; Acts 1:1).[11] In the last third of the first century, the church generally struggled to survive in an increasingly hostile political environment. Luke, not unlike other New Testament writers of this period and after,[12] seeks perhaps to assuage Rome by allowing his theological framework to be determined by the assumption of a Roman-centered world.[13] In this process of secularization, the Lukan vision of universalism is undermined by this seeming theological emphasis upon Europe. Of course, we must remember that the New Testament's final vision of the holy remnant (Rev. 7:9) is consistent with Luke's notion of racial pluralism as shown in Acts 13:1. In Acts, two Africans are mentioned as part of the leadership team of the Church of Antioch: namely, Simeon, who was called *Niger* (Latin: the black man), and Lucius of Cyrene (a province or a city in Africa). Both Revelation 7 and Acts 13 indicate that persons of all nations and races constitute the people of God in the history of salvation.

Another instance of secularization in the New Testament has to do with the Eurocentric bias that has accentuated the movement of the gospel geographically from Jerusalem to points north. This geographical progression is then translated into modern maps of New Testament lands that de-Africanize the entire New Testament. The result is that New Testament scholarship limits itself to focusing upon the Greco-Roman world. Hence modern readers of the Bible take it for granted that maps of New Testament lands appropriately eliminate the continent of Africa. Even the modern creation of the so-called Middle East can only be seen as an extension of this Western tendency to de-Africanize this section of the world. Thus it has trivialized the ancient contribution of Africa in the shaping of the peoples and cultures of the entire region. Clearly, we are dealing with a modern ideological set of hermeneutical assumptions that suggests that nothing good has ever come out of Africa. What we must remember is that this thinking constitutes nothing short of fraudulent historiography on the part of Eurocentric Bible scholars. This in fact is another form of secularization

because modern Eurocentric translators and interpreters of the New Testament have tended to allow
secular ideological presuppositions to govern their
exegesis and interpretation. The post-Enlightenment,
systematic theories of race and thus racism have been
tacitly affirmed and strengthened by the acquies-
cence of Eurocentric Bible scholars who ignore or
trivialize ancient black culture as reflected in the Bible.

Finally, I want to stress once again that the biblical world predated any systematic notion of races
and theories of racism. In the foregoing discussion,
I have tried to examine authors of ancient biblical
narratives in order to reveal surprises that constitute a basis for interrogating modern-day mainline
churches and synagogues afresh on their "readings"
and subjective modernist "applications" of Scripture.
Secularization in the New Testament is a process that
needs much fuller exploration in terms of its racial
dimensions. At one level, it highlights the continuing
ambiguity of race in the New Testament. At another
level, it confronts us today with a challenge to search
for more adequate modes of hermeneutics that can be
used to demonstrate that the New Testament—even
as it stands locked into the socioreligious framework
of the Greco-Roman world—is relevant to blacks and
other marginalized peoples. Of all the mandates that
confront the church in the world today, the mandate

of world community predicated on a renewed commitment to pluralism and the attendant acknowledgment of the integrity of all racial groups constitutes an urgent agenda for Bible scholars and the laity alike. It is an agenda far too long neglected in the vast array of Eurocentric theological and ecclesial traditions that continue to marginalize people of color throughout the world.

# *Notes*

## INTRODUCTION

1  See Frank Snowden, *Before Color Prejudice: The Ancient View of Blacks* (Cambridge, MA: Harvard University Press, 1983), 14–17, 43–46; and Nicholas F. Gier, "The Color of Sin / The Color of Skin: Ancient Color Blindness and the Philosophical Origins of Modern Racism," *Journal of Religious Thought* 46, no. 1 (Summer–Fall 1989): 42–52.

2  See Charles B. Copher, "Three Thousand Years of Biblical Interpretation with Reference to Black Peoples," *Journal of the Interdenominational Theological Center* 13, no. 2 (Spring 1986): 225–46; see also his "The Black Presence in the Old Testament," in *Stony the Road We Trod: African American Biblical Interpretation*, ed. Cain Hope Felder (1991; Minneapolis: Fortress, 2021), 165–84.

3  Cornel West, *Prophetic Fragments* (Grand Rapids, MI: William B. Eerdmans, 1988), 100.

4  G. Johannes Botterweck and Helmer Ringgren, eds., *Theological Dictionary of the Old Testament* (hereafter TDOT), 6 vols. (Grand Rapids, MI: William B. Eerdmans, 1974–84), 2:426–29, s.v. "*góy.*"

5  D. Goitein, *Jews and Arabs: Their Contacts through the Ages* (New York: Schocken Books, 1964), 19–21.

6 *Aithiops* (burnt-face) is the most frequent translation of *Cush* found in the Septuagint; usually it designates Africans of dark pigmentation and Negroid features. It was used as early as Homer (*Odyssey* 19.246ff.). While *Aithiops* in ancient biblical and classical texts refers specifically to Ethiopians, the term also identifies Africans, regardless of race (see Frank M. Snowden Jr., *Blacks in Antiquity: Ethiopians in the Greco-Roman Experience* [Cambridge, MA: Belknap Press of Harvard University Press, 1970], 118–19).

7 G. E. Mendenhall employs the term *secularization* in this sense in George A. Buttrick et al., eds., *The Interpreter's Dictionary of the Bible* (hereafter IDB), 4 vols. (New York: Abingdon, 1962), 2:77, s.v. "election."

## THE CURSE OF HAM

1 Claus Westermann, *Genesis 1–11: A Commentary* (Minneapolis: Augsburg, 1984), 459. The Priestly (P) tradition may be dated 550–450 BCE, beginning in the exilic period (Babylonian captivity) but extending into the postexilic period where the redaction evidently continued.

2 Westermann, 482.

3 Westermann, 486.

4 Gene Rice, "The Curse That Never Was (Genesis 9:18–27)," *Journal of Religious Thought* 29 (1972): 13.

5 Westermann, *Genesis*, 47.

6 Westermann, 54.

7 J. Oluminde Lucas, *The Religion of the Yorubas* (Lagos: C. M. S. Bookshop, 1948; cited in Cheikh Anta Diop, *The African Origin of Civilization: Myth or Reality?* [New York: Lawrence Hill, 1974], 184–99). See also Robert E. Hood, "Creation Myths in Nigeria," *Journal of Religious Thought* 45 (Winter–Spring 1989): 70–84.

8  Rice, "Curse," 11–12; Westermann, *Genesis*, 488–89; and Ephraim Isaac, "Genesis, Judaism and the 'Sons of Ham,'" *Slavery and Abolition: A Journal of Comparative Studies* 1, no. 1 (May 1980): 4–5.

9  Rice ("Curse," 7–8) suggests that the passage contains two parallel but different traditions—one universal (Gen. 9:18–19a; cf. 5:32; 6:10; 7:13; 10:1; 1 Chron. 1:4) and the other limited to Palestine and more parochial (Gen. 9:20–27; see also Gen. 10:21).

10  Westermann, *Genesis*, 484.

11  *Midrash Bereshith Rabbah* (London: Soncino, 1939), 1:293 (cited in Rice, "Curse," 17, 25).

12  See Isaac, "Genesis," 19.

13  Rice, "Curse," 26n116.

14  Finis Jennings Dake, *Dake's Annotated Reference Bible* (Lawrenceville, GA: Dake Bible Sales, 1981), 8, 9, 36, 40. One of my African seminarians, who had been given *Dake's Annotated* by fundamentalist American missionaries, innocently presented me with a gift copy for study and comment!

## OLD TESTAMENT GENEALOGIES

1  Martin Noth, *A History of Pentateuchal Traditions*, trans. Bernhard W. Anderson (Chico, CA: Scholars Press, 1981), 21–23, 28, and the translator's supplement on 262–63. See also Otto Eissfeldt, *The Old Testament: An Introduction* (New York: Harper and Row, 1965), 184.

2  IDB 4:311, s.v. "Sabeans."

3  The postexilic Priestly (P) redaction accounts for the order Shem, Ham, Japheth (omitting Canaan) in Genesis 10:1 as well as for the inversion of this order in the subsequent verses: for example, the sons of Japheth (Gen. 10:2), the sons of Ham (Gen. 10:6), and "To Shem

also, the father of all the children of Eber (Hebrew)"
(Gen. 10:21).

4 Rice, "Curse," 16 (emphasis mine).

## THE NARRATIVE ABOUT MIRIAM AND AARON

1 Contra B. W. Anderson's note on Numbers 12:1 in *The New Oxford Annotated Bible* (New York: Oxford University Press, 1977), 179: "The term Cushite apparently includes Midianites and other Arabic peoples (Hab. 3:7)."

2 Cain Hope Felder, "Racial Motifs in the Biblical Narratives," in *Troubling Biblical Waters: Race, Class, and Family* (Maryknoll, NY: Orbis, 1989), 42.

3 Randall C. Bailey, "Beyond Identification: The Use of Africans in Old Testament Poetry and Narratives," in Felder, *Stony the Road We Trod*, 185–206.

4 Isaac, "Genesis," 3–17.

5 Sergew Hable Sellassie, *Ancient and Medieval Ethiopian History to 1270* (Addis Ababa: United Printers, 1972), 96; R. A. Morrisey, *Colored People and Bible History* (Hammond, IN: W. B. Conkey, 1925), especially chaps. 1, 2; and Edward Ullendorf, *Ethiopia and the Bible* (London: Oxford University Press, 1968), 6–8.

6 Snowden, *Blacks in Antiquity*, 115–17; Diop, *African Origin*, 220–21; and Alan Gardiner, *Egypt of the Pharaohs* (New York: Oxford University Press, 1974).

7 Copher, "Three Thousand Years."

## THE DOCTRINE OF ELECTION

1 Gerhard von Rad, *Old Testament Theology*, trans. D. M. G. Stalker, 2 vols. (New York: Harper and Row, 1962), 1:7; 2:322.

2   Von Rad, 1:118, 178; TDOT 2:78, s.v. "*bāchar*"; and IDB 2:76, s.v. "election."

3   TDOT 2:82, s.v. "*bāchar*."

4   TDOT 2:83, s.v. "*bāchar*."

5   So IDB 2:79, s.v. "election"; and George F. Moore, *Judaism* (Cambridge, MA: Harvard University Press, 1932), 2:95. But cf. M. Rosenbaum and A. M. Silverman, *Pentateuch with Targum Onkelos, Haphtaroth and Rashi's Commentary: Genesis, Deuteronomy* (New York: Hebrew Publishing, n.d.), 56, 195.

6   Von Rad, *Old Testament Theology*, 1:178, 223.

7   TDOT 2:78, s.v. "*bāchar*."

8   Moore, *Judaism*, 95.

9   Rudolf Bultmann, *Theology and the New Testament* (London: SCM, 1965), 1:97.

10  Isa. 43:20 (LXX), *to genos mou to eklekton* = M.T., *'ammi beḥiri*.

11  W. Bauer, *A Greek-English Lexicon of the New Testament*, trans. and ed. W. E. Arnot and F. W. Gingrich (Chicago: University of Chicago Press, 1957), 242, s.v. "*eklektos*."

## SECULARIZATION IN THE NEW TESTAMENT

1   In 1 Clement 7, "the limits of the west" (*epi to terma tēs duseōs*) designates Spain (i.e., Spain is at the western limits of Rome; see *Apostolic Fathers*, Loeb Classical Library [Cambridge, MA: Harvard University Press, 1975], 1:16). See Romans 15:28 and the analysis of it in Ernst Käsemann, *Commentary on Romans*, trans. and ed. Geoffrey W. Bromiley (Grand Rapids, MI: William B. Eerdmans, 1980), 402.

2   Luke's Acts of the Apostles outlines this scheme quite decidedly: Jerusalem (Acts 2), Antioch (Acts 12), Athens (Acts 17), and Rome (Acts 28). See Werner Georg

Kümmel, *Introduction to the New Testament*, trans. Howard C. Kee, rev. ed. (Nashville: Abingdon, 1975), 164f.

3   Vincent Taylor, *The Gospel according to St. Mark* (New York: St. Martin's Press, 1966), 598; and Werner H. Kelber, ed., *The Passion of Mark* (Philadelphia: Fortress, 1976), 120n, 155, 166.

4   The good reputations of the centurion in Luke 7:2ff. and Cornelius the centurion in Acts 10:1, 22 are intentional designs by Luke (see F. J. Foakes-Jackson and Kirsopp Lake, eds., *The Acts of the Apostles* [Grand Rapids, MI: Baker Book House, 1979], 4:112; and Ernst Haenchen, *The Acts of the Apostles: A Commentary* [Philadelphia: Westminster, 1971], 346, 349).

5   Haenchen, *Acts of the Apostles*, 309.

6   Haenchen, 314.

7   Haenchen, 315. Similarly, Martin Hengel, *Acts and the History of the Earliest Christianity* (Philadelphia: Fortress, 1980), 79.

8   Irenaeus (120–202 CE) reports that the Ethiopian became a missionary "to the regions of Ethiopia," and Epiphanius (315–403 CE) says that he preached in Arabia Felix and on the coasts of the Red Sea. Unfortunately, there are no records of Ethiopian Christianity until the fourth century (see Foakes-Jackson and Lake, *Acts*, 4:98).

9   Irenaeus cites the text as if the variant reading is part of the text (*Adv. Haer.* 3.12.8; see Alexander Roberts and James Donaldson, eds., *The Ante-Nicene Fathers* [Grand Rapids, MI: William B. Eerdmans, 1981], 1:433; see also *The Western Text*, *The Antiochian Text*, and *Textus Receptus*; the English Authorized Version includes verse 37). Foakes-Jackson and Lake (*Acts*, 4:98) suggest that the principal significance of verse 37 is that it is "perhaps the earliest form of the baptismal creed. It is also remarkable that it is an expansion of the baptismal

formula 'in the name of Jesus Christ,' not of the trinitarian formula."

10  "Simeon the 'black' may have come from Africa and may possibly be Simon of Cyrene" (C. S. C. Williams, *The Acts of the Apostles* [New York: Harper and Row, 1957], 154). Haenchen (*Acts of the Apostles*, 395n2) reminds us that 1 Corinthians 12:28f. lists first apostles, prophets, and teachers as persons endowed with charismata, and these constituted a charismatic office in Pauline churches.

11  See Hans Conzelmann, *The Theology of St. Luke*, trans. Geoffrey Buswell (New York: Harper and Row, 1960), 138–41; and Richard J. Cassidy, *Jesus, Politics, and Society* (Maryknoll, NY: Orbis, 1978), 128–30.

12  Notably the pastorals (1 and 2 Timothy and Titus) and 1 Peter; cf. Rom. 13:1–5.

13  It should be noted, however, that the extent of the political-apologetic element in Luke–Acts continues to be at the storm center of New Testament debate. See Cassidy, *Jesus, Politics, and Society*; Cassidy, *Society and Politics in the Acts of the Apostles* (Maryknoll, NY: Orbis, 1987); Donald Juel, *Luke-Acts: The Promise of History* (Atlanta: John Knox, 1983); and Jack T. Sanders, *The Jews in Luke-Acts* (Philadelphia: Fortress, 1987).